iPlayMusic®

Beginner Guitar Lessons
Level 1

For more information about iPlayMusic, Inc., please email us at info@iplaymusic.com.

www.iPlayMusic.com

Author: Quincy Carroll
Editing: Quincy Carroll, Noel Rabinowitz
Cover design: Chris Canote
Graphic design: Karyn Nelson Designs
Illustrations: Mike Biegel
Photography: Luke O'Byrne

Order No. IP10036
ISBN-10: 0-9760487-5-2
ISBN-13: 978-0-9760487-5-6

Exclusive Distributors:
Music Sales Corporation
257 Park Avenue South, New York, NY 10010 USA
Music Sales Limited
14-15 Berners Street, London W1T 3LJ England
Music Sales Pty. Limited
120 Rothschild Street, Rosebery, Sydney, NSW 2018, Australia

Printed in the United States of America by
Vicks Lithograph and Printing Corporation

The vision of iPlayMusic, Inc. is to deliver the unique joy and experience of making music to novice and non-musicians. In **Beginner Guitar Lessons Level 1** we present the essentials you need to know in order to start playing songs right away.

iPlayMusic, Inc. was formed by a group of friends with 20 years of combined playing and teaching experience. The award-winning iPlayMusic teaching method has gained critical acclaim among reviewers, industry experts, and seasoned musicians. Our teaching method has been refined over the years through conversations with customers, friends, instructors, advanced players, and absolute beginners. Based on this research, we decided early on to focus on teaching people the skills they need to play songs as soon as possible. We hope you will pick up skills from this product that help you experience the joy of playing songs on guitar!

How to Use the Book, DVD, and iPod Videos

This book is designed to be used in combination with the accompanying DVD and iPod videos. For sections where we have included video, you should read through that section and any prior sections before watching the videos.

The DVD has two sides. The side labeled "DVD Video" contains the DVD video, which is playable on any standard DVD player. The side labeled "iPod Videos" contains the iPod videos in a folder called "Drag to iTunes."

Playing the DVD. To play the DVD, simply insert the DVD, with the "DVD Video" side up, into any standard DVD player. If the DVD does not play automatically, then you may have inserted the disk on the wrong side. In this case simply eject the disk, flip it over, and re-insert the DVD.

Exporting the iPod videos. These specially formatted videos are designed for use with your video iPod. Once exported to your iPod, you will have access to all the video lessons and songs, so you can learn and play anytime, anywhere! To export the iPod videos to your video iPod, follow these six steps:

1. Insert the DVD, with the "iPod Videos" side up, into your computer's DVD drive. If your DVD player software launches, then you may have inserted the disk on the wrong side. In this case simply quit the DVD player software, eject the disk, flip it over, and re-insert the DVD.

2. Open the disk by double-clicking. If you have a Macintosh computer, double-click the "Beginner Guitar Level 1" DVD icon on your desktop to open it. If you have a Windows computer, go to "My Computer," find your DVD-Rom drive, and double-click it to open it.

3. Launch iTunes.

4. Create a playlist in iTunes.

5. Drag and drop the folder called "Drag to iTunes" from the DVD into the playlist you created in iTunes. All of the videos will now copy to this playlist.

6. Drag and drop the playlist onto your video iPod.

Table of Contents

BASICS

STYLES
Rock, Blues, Country, Metal and Punk

Table of Contents

iPlayMusic®

Beginner Guitar Lessons
BASICS

Before we get into the lessons, it is important to understand some basic terminology and the layout of your guitar.

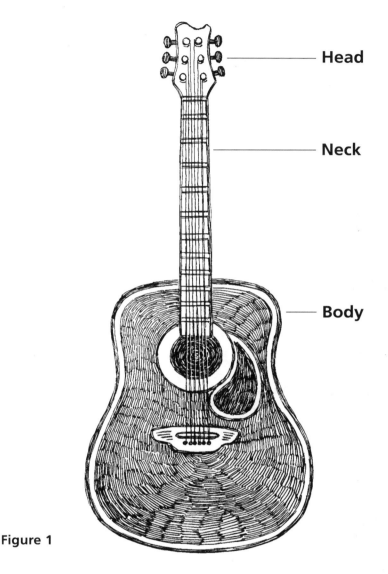

Head

Neck

Body

Figure 1

Guitar Neck

This is the long part of the guitar that the strings run across. The front of the neck is called the **fretboard**.

Guitar Body

This is the largest part of the guitar. Guitar bodies have many different shapes, sizes, and wood types that create a variety of tones. If you have an **acoustic guitar** or *hollow body* **electric guitar**, then it's the part that is hollowed out. If you have an **electric guitar** with a *solid body*, the sound is converted to an electric signal through your guitar pickups that are located under the strings on the body of the guitar. The signal is sent to your amplifier via the guitar cable, and the amplifier then boosts the signal and adds its own character to the sound.

Guitar Anatomy

Guitar Frets

Guitar frets are the **metal strips** on the fretboard of the guitar neck. Frets are spaced apart from each other and span all the way up the neck. Frets exist so that when you press down on a string at a particular position of the neck, the string makes a specific tone. **The higher up** the neck you go, the higher the "pitch" of the sound will be.

VIDEO: *watch Video 1 "Guitar Anatomy"*

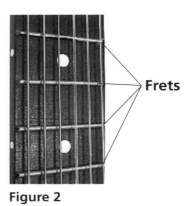

Frets

Figure 2

Fret and String Numbering

In this book and in the accompanying videos, we number the frets and strings for simplicity.

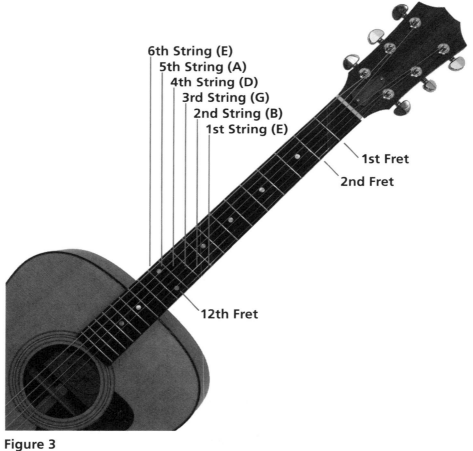

6th String (E)
5th String (A)
4th String (D)
3rd String (G)
2nd String (B)
1st String (E)

1st Fret
2nd Fret

12th Fret

Figure 3

Tuning Keys

There are six tuning keys on the head of your guitar. By turning these keys, you can adjust the tension of the strings on the guitar. By tightening, you can raise the pitch of a particular string. By loosening, you can lower the pitch.

Tuning Keys

Figure 4

Guitar Bridge

The bridge is located at the base of the guitar body. It holds the end of the strings to the guitar on the body.

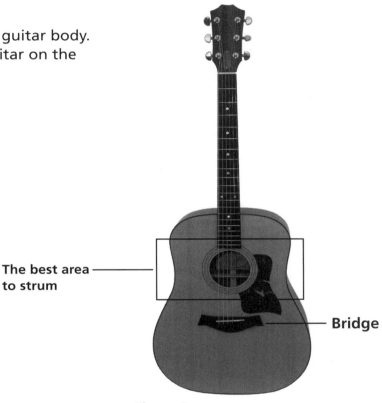

The best area to strum

Bridge

Figure 5

For the best (most resonant) tone, the strings of the guitar should be strummed in-between the base of the neck of the guitar and the bridge of the guitar (the boxed area in figure 5).

These are the essential parts of the guitar that we will be discussing in this book. There is a lot of other guitar-specific and musical terminology that we've chosen to omit, because we want to keep things as simple and straightforward as possible, so you can start having fun and playing right away.

How to Hold Your Guitar

Body Positioning

First, find a comfortable place to sit where you can have your legs in front of you and your feet on the ground. This is your **"foundation"** that the guitar will rest on.

Next, make sure you're sitting comfortably and have good posture.

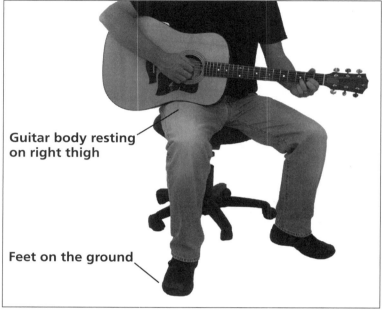

Guitar body resting on right thigh

Feet on the ground

Figure 6

Playing guitar for hours will eventually strain your back if you do not maintain a nice **upright** sitting posture. Pick up your guitar and place the back of the guitar against your stomach. If you are **right-handed**, the guitar neck should be pointing towards your left. Rest the guitar body on your right thigh.

Now place your left hand around the guitar neck and place your right arm around the body so that your hand is lying by the strings. Adjust your body positioning as necessary, so that you are completely comfortable.

Hand Positioning

If you're **left-handed**, don't worry, Jimi Hendrix was left-handed! You basically have two options here. The first option is to buy a right-handed guitar and re-string it, so that the order of the strings in figure 3 is reversed. The second option you have is to buy a left-handed guitar.

If you're **right-handed**, you will use your left hand, as shown below, to construct chords.

As you can see in figure 7, the left-hand fingers are bent and pressing down on the strings on the fretboard. The back of the neck is curved, so that your hand molds into the shape of the neck. In this image, the thumb is arching over the top of the neck. This is a common thumb position for constructing chords.

Figure 7

It is also OK to **press your thumb** into the back of the guitar neck when constructing chords, although this is more common when playing scales. Try both thumb positions and use the one that is most comfortable for you.

Don't worry about what strings your left-hand fingers are pressing down on at this point. We are just trying to get you familiar with the hand and finger positioning.

Figure 8

For the chords you will learn in this section it is very important that you have only your fingertips touching the strings. If any other part of your fingers are touching the strings when you construct a chord, it will sound muffled or muted. **To be clear**, there are many instances, such as when constructing barre chords, that it is perfectly fine, in fact desirable, to allow your entire finger to lay across the strings. However, **for the basic chords** in this lesson, it is important to only press down on the strings with your fingertips.

Right Hand/Arm

This is the hand that you will use to **"strum"** the strings to make the different chord sounds. Remember to position your hand so that when you strike the strings, you are strumming in the boxed area of figure 5. This is the most resonant sounding part of the guitar.

Figure 9

Bring your right arm over the guitar. Your **right bicep** should be resting on the top of the body of the guitar. Your **hand** should be positioned directly above the soundhole in the guitar. This is where the sound is produced. Figure 9 shows the correct right-hand/arm positioning.

VIDEO: *watch Video 2 "How to Hold Your Guitar"*

Guitar Pick

The guitar pick is used with the strumming hand to either pick the strings individually or strum them all at once to play chords. Picks come in many shapes and sizes. The **thickness** of the pick is usually marked on the pick. Thickness ranges from thin to heavy. Medium is a good thickness to start with, but you should try a few different gauges and see what thickness you like.

Not all guitarists use a pick. Mark Knopfler, the guitarist from Dire Straits, is perhaps the most famous lead guitarist in the pop music world to use his fingers, rather than a pick, when soloing. Classical, folk, and flamenco guitarists also use fingerstyle rather than a pick to play the guitar. For the most part, it is easier for beginners to produce a nice smooth sound with the pick, so we suggest that you learn how to play with a pick first and then venture off into the world of fingerstyle once you are more advanced.

The guitar pick is held with the **thumb and index finger** of the strumming hand. Grip the fat end of the pick between your thumb and index finger. The pointed part of the pick should be facing in towards the strings. See figure 10.

Striking the strings with the pick

Now that you understand how to hold the pick, you should practice striking individual strings on the guitar. Make sure that you have a firm grip, and then strike the 6th string, making sure that you strike the string with the very **tip** of the pick (about 1/4 of the pick's surface area). In general, if you strike the strings with the same intensity, **the more tip** you have exposed the louder the chord will be. Try striking the 6th string lightly and then more firmly to notice the different tones you can generate. **Avoid** striking the string so hard that it buzzes. This is a sure sign that you're picking too hard.

Figure 10

Figure 11 illustrates how we number each finger when explaining which fingers to place on the fretboard when playing notes and constructing chords.

Figure 11

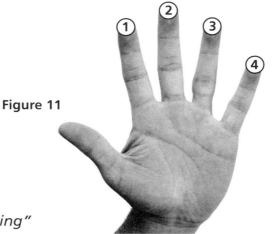

VIDEO: *watch Video 3 "String, Fret, and Finger Numbering"*
watch Video 4 "Making Sound"

Tuning the guitar is **critical**, because nothing you play will sound "right" if the guitar is not in tune. If your guitar is out of tune or tuned incorrectly it will make a perfectly constructed chord sound bad.

There are **many ways** to tune your guitar:

1. With an electronic tuner
2. With tuning software
3. By ear with a tuning fork
4. By ear with another guitar or reference note

The easiest and most accurate way to tune your guitar is with an **electronic tuner** or with tuning software. Electronic tuners typically work for both acoustic or electric guitars, although this is not always the case. An acoustic guitar tuner will have a built-in microphone, to pick up the sound. Electric guitar tuners usually have a 1/4" instrument cable input for the guitar. Most tuners have both a built-in microphone and a 1/4" instrument cable input. We highly recommend that you purchase an electronic tuner, such as the Boss TU-15 Chromatic Tuner.

Figure 12

There is also some great free or inexpensive software available for tuning the guitar. Most software tuning products range in cost from $10 to $20 and work with standard computer sound cards and microphones.

Although electronic tuners and software tuners are great tools, we suggest that you learn to tune your guitar by ear to a reference note. **This will help** you to train your ear, so you can quickly tune during a live performance or when you don't have an electronic tuner nearby.

You can also try tuning with a **tuning fork**. A tuning fork will provide you with a reference tone. You can buy tuning forks at any musical instrument retailer. The most common tuning fork for guitarists generates an A (440) **reference tone**, so you can tune the 5th string (A). In order to generate a tone with the tuning fork, you should lightly tap it against a hard surface and then press the non-forked end against the body of your guitar. This will cause the tone to resonate throughout the guitar body, so that it is louder.

Tune your 5th string to the A tuning fork's tone by picking the "open" 5th (A) string ("open" means that you just play the string without pressing down on any frets) while listening to the tone of the tuning fork. **Adjust the tuning key** for your 5th string by turning it in either direction until the tone of the picked string and the tuning fork are identical.

Tuning Your Guitar

Once your 5th string is in tune, you can tune all the rest of the strings on your guitar. Start with the 6th (E) string.   This is the fattest string of the six. It's also the string at the top of the guitar (see figure 3 for reference).

Press your index finger on the 5th fret, 6th string. **Make sure** that you press firmly and that your index finger is close to the edge of the fret, almost touching it. If your string is buzzing as you pick it, then either you are not pressing firmly enough, or your finger is not positioned close enough to the edge of the fret.

Pick the 6th string with your index finger pressing down on the 5th fret, 6th string and then pick the "open" 5th (A) string.   Compare the two tones. The pitch of the 5th fret, 6th string should be the same sound as the open 5th (A) string. If it is not the exact same sound then turn the 6th string's tuning key so that the sound is the same. Now your 6th and 5th strings are tuned.

Repeat this step, but this time place your index finger on the 5th fret of the 5th string. Pick that string and then pick the open 4th string. They should sound the same. If they don't, turn the tuning key for the 4th string so that the 4th string sounds like the 5th. Be careful to turn the correct tuning key.

Continue the same process from the 4th string to the 3rd string. When you get to tuning the 2nd string there is a slight change. To tune the 2nd (B) string, place your index finger on the 4th fret, 3rd string (instead of the 5th fret). Now pick the 3rd string and then pick the 2nd string. If the 2nd string does not sound like the 3rd, then turn the 2nd string's tuning key so that the 2nd string sounds like the 3rd.

Finally, for the 1st (E) string, move your index finger back to the 5th fret on the 2nd string. Then pick the 2nd and 1st strings. The open 1st string should sound exactly like the 5th fret, 2nd string. If it doesn't, then turn the 1st string's tuning key so that it sounds like the 2nd string.

Okay, that is probably going to be the toughest part of learning to play guitar. We recommend you buy an electronic tuner, but knowing how to tune the guitar by ear will be extremely valuable, especially in live playing situations or at times when you don't have access to a tuner.

VIDEO: *watch Video 5 "Tuning the Guitar"*
         watch Video 6 "Practice Playing Strings"

Now for the fun stuff. In this section we will teach you the basic chords you need to know to play the songs you love. So let's get started!

Before we move on to chord construction, here are some basic tips that will help you sound better.

1. Press firmly

Be sure you press each finger down so that it firmly presses the string against the fretboard. This will ensure the sound of the string is clean and does not buzz. If you don't push the string down hard enough you will hear a buzzing or a muffled sound.

2. Close to the fret

In general (this is not always the case), make sure that your finger is as close to the fret as possible without actually touching the fret. This will ensure that the string does not buzz or sound muffled when played.

3. One finger per string

Be sure that only one finger touches each string. Oftentimes you will find one finger slightly touching a neighboring string. This is particularly common with the more difficult chords (like the G Major chord). This is one other cause of muffled or buzzing strings. Take some time after constructing the chord to make sure that each finger is only touching the necessary strings and not resting on neighboring strings.

4. Relax

Relax your hand so that it is comfortable when constructing the chord. Re-position your wrist for each chord so that you are comfortable and so that your fingers can sustain their position (without cramping) while you strum.

On the following pages you will find pictures and **videos** (contained on the DVD) that explain the finger placement for three chords: A Major, G Major, and D Major.

These are three of the most widely used chords in popular songs today.

By learning to play **just these three chords** you will know the building blocks of many popular songs by some of the biggest recording artists.

Look at each chord diagram closely. Spend some time positioning your fingers to look like the images. Try constructing these chords yourself, strumming them, and listening to how they sound.

If you are having trouble, don't panic. Just play the **chord videos** on the DVD to watch the instructor construct the chords step by step.

VIDEO: *watch Video 7 "Constructing Chords"*

Basic Chords

A Major

VIDEO: *watch Video 8 "A Major Chord"*

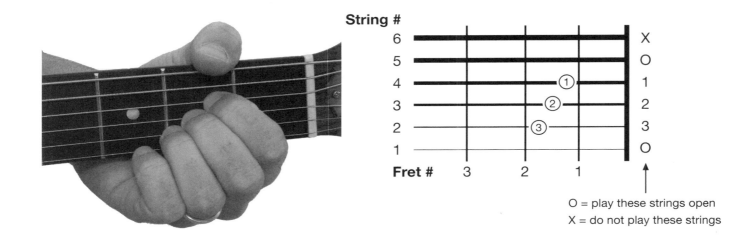

G Major

VIDEO: *watch Video 9 "G Major Chord"*

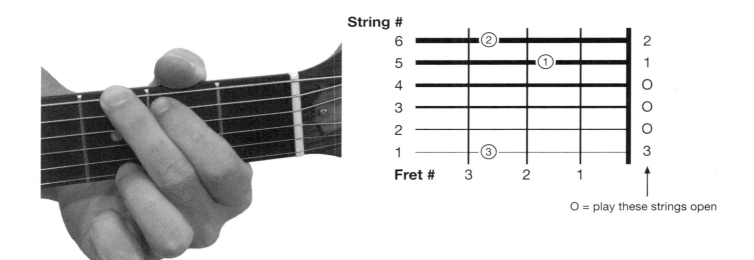

D Major

VIDEO: *watch Video 10 "D Major Chord"*

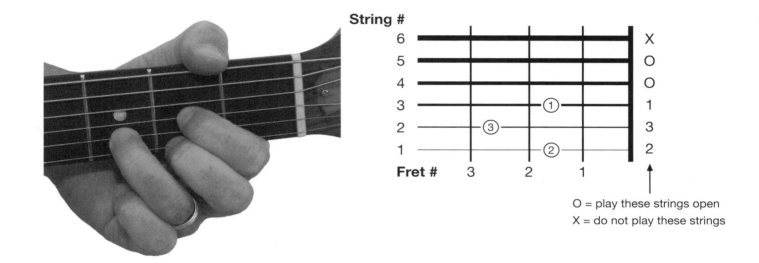

String #

6				X
5				O
4				O
3		①		1
2	③			3
1		②		2

Fret #   3   2   1

O = play these strings open
X = do not play these strings

Strumming Patterns

Now that you are comfortable with A Major, D Major, and G Major, it's time to start making music. There are **three fundamentals** you will need in order to play songs:

1. **Chord construction (which we just covered)**

2. **Strumming patterns**

3. **Transitions**

Knowing the chords is the first step in playing music. If you're right-handed, you use your **left hand** to construct chords and your **right hand** to strum the guitar. When you strum chords, you play the strings of your guitar with your picking hand either with a downstroke or an upstroke. **Strumming patterns** are combinations of down- and upstrokes that make rhythmic sense. Here are the **basic rules** to remember when strumming the guitar:

1. Don't break your wrist. When strumming the guitar, over 90% of the motion in your right arm should be in twisting your forearm, not breaking your wrist. Your wrist should remain firm and not flimsy. If your wrist is flimsy, your strumming will sound sloppy. Most of the up-down motion of your hand should be controlled by turning your entire forearm. Use your elbow to help your forearm move up and down.

2. Maintain a firm grip on the pick. Make sure that you grasp the pick firmly, or else you will not be able to generate a nice tone from the guitar. Refer back to page 12 for a refresher on proper pick technique.

3. Your arm is a windshield wiper. Visually, you should think of your arm as a windshield wiper that is moving up and down at the same pace, over and over. Don't ever stop your arm from moving up and down. Keep a nice rhythm. The key is to only play the up- and downstrokes when you want to generate sound but to always keep your arm moving up and down at a constant and steady rhythm, just like a windshield wiper.

In this section you will learn how to play two popular strumming patterns.

A **strumming pattern** consists of downstrokes and upstrokes.

A **downstroke** is played by strumming the guitar strings from the top of the guitar to the bottom – or from the 6th (low E) string to the 1st (high E) string. We will represent a downstroke with a down arrow:

↓

An **upstroke** is played by strumming the guitar strings from the bottom of the guitar to the top – or from the 1st (high E) string to the 6th (low E) string. We will represent an upstroke with an up arrow:

↑

Remember to think of your strumming hand as a windshield wiper, or a pendulum. **A dashed arrow** will represent the direction your arm should be moving as you swing your arm up and down without hitting the strings.

If you need further instruction, or these concepts seem a bit confusing, please watch the "Strumming Basics" video and then make sure to watch the videos at the end of this section for an in-depth explanation of each pattern from the instructor.

VIDEO: *watch Video 11 "Strumming Basics"*
watch Video 12 "Practice Drill"

With just the following **two strumming patterns** you will have the ability to play many popular songs. Let's get started.

Strumming pattern 1 is a very classic strumming pattern that can be used to play a number of songs.

Strumming pattern: Down, down, up, up, down, up.

Try strumming pattern 1 with any of the three chords you've already learned.

If you need further instruction on strumming pattern 1, please watch the video for an explanation from the instructor.

VIDEO: *watch Video 13 "Strumming Pattern 1"*

Strumming pattern 2 is a slight variation on strumming pattern 1, because it adds one upstroke and introduces a "swing" feel to the pattern.

Strumming pattern: Down, up, down, up, up, down, up.

(SWING)

Again, try strumming pattern 2 with any of the three chords you've already learned.

VIDEO: *watch Video 14 "Strumming Pattern 2"*

Transitions

Now you know how to play two strumming patterns with just one chord. The next step is to play these strumming patterns while transitioning **between chords**.

The most important thing to remember when learning how to transition between chords is to start out SLOWLY.

Try playing a few downstrokes with the D chord and then switch to the G chord. Try to keep your strumming arm moving at a constant rhythm as you transition between chords. Slow down as much as you need to in order to ensure that your strumming arm never skips a beat. Even if it feels painfully slow, this is the only way to become proficient at changing between chords.

Another very important thing to remember is to keep your strumming arm moving at a constant, steady motion, just like a windshield wiper. You'll be amazed at how quickly you can increase the speed (or tempo) of your strumming arm if you start slowly and build up.

The trick to making transitions sound smooth is to play some open high strings or muted strings as you make your transition from one chord to another. **This ensures** that you maintain the rhythmic sound of the strumming pattern as you transition between chords. For a more in-depth explanation of this transition trick, **watch the videos** on the DVD to learn from the instructor.

VIDEO: *watch Video 15 "Chord Transitions"*
watch Video 16 "Practicing Chords"

It's important to work on keeping rhythm and tempo as you play strumming patterns and transition between chords. Remember to start slowly. Don't try to go really fast until you are totally comfortable at a slower tempo. Work your way up to a comfortable speed. You'll soon find that with just a little practice you'll be playing at any speed you want with any chords and strumming patterns. Eventually you'll even start coming up with your own patterns!

There are two important things to remember when you practice your guitar:

1. Start slowly

Remember not to rush when you learn something new. It is always tempting to try to start playing a new chord or strumming pattern at full speed, because you are excited and want to hear it the way it is supposed to sound. If you slow down and spend an hour or so nailing the chord construction, strumming pattern, and transitions, you will have that song under your belt for the rest of your life. Conversely, if you try to play it at full speed right away and get frustrated, you may never learn it.

2. Play with a metronome

If possible, always have a metronome with you when you practice. A metronome is a device that plays a "click" sound to the tempo (or speed) that you specify. Practice your transitions and strumming patterns to the beat of a metronome. That way you will develop some discipline around maintaining the "windshield wiper" rhythm with your strumming arm. Set the metronome to a slow tempo at first and then gradually increase the tempo until you are up to speed.

If you remember these two important rules, you will have **productive practice sessions**, and you'll be playing like a pro sooner than you can imagine.

This approach may seem slow and methodical, but it is **amazing how quickly** you can get up to speed if you start slowly. It is an exponential increase – suddenly, one day you can play fast. It seems to happen overnight!

Your **fingers** are going to hurt when you first start playing. This is actually a good sign, and eventually you will develop calluses that keep the tips of your fingers protected. This can take a little time, but we recommend playing until your fingers start to get uncomfortable. When this happens take a break. There is no need to overstimulate your fingertips, so just take your time. The pain will go away and you will eventually find that you will be able to play for longer and longer periods of time with no pain at all.

Your **hands**, especially the hand you use to construct chords, may also get sore. This is very normal. To strengthen your hand we recommend that you **watch** the video that explains how to strengthen your left hand.

VIDEO: *watch Video 17 "Finger Strength"*

Remember to set a time every day for practice. Even if it's only 15 minutes. This is enough time to develop **"muscle memory."** Eventually your hands will just know what to do. It's a strange phenomenon, but the more you practice, the more you start remembering with your hands instead of your brain. When you get to this point, playing becomes really fun!

Songs

Well, you did it!

You've learned enough to **start playing** the songs you love. You will now be able to wow your friends, family, and loved ones.

Following are a couple of songs that use the chords we have taught you above – A Major, G Major, and D Major. By combining both the chords in the right order (arrangement) and the strumming patterns you've learned, you will soon start recognizing that you are playing some very popular songs that everyone knows.

FIRST SONG

Sloop John B.
Made popular by the Beach Boys and the Kingston Trio

This song originated in the Bahamas in the early twentieth century and was covered by the Beach Boys on their album *Pet Sounds*. It tells the story of a traveler who has a rowdy evening in Nassau and his desire to return home.

VIDEO: *watch videos 18-21 "Sloop John B."*

SECOND SONG

Corrina, Corrina
Made popular by Bob Dylan and Eric Clapton

Also known as "Alberta," this song has been an American folk standard for over 100 years. A lament about an unfaithful or lost lover, "Corrina, Corrina" has been adapted and recorded by multiple artists, including Bob Dylan and Eric Clapton.

VIDEO: *watch videos 22-25 "Corrina, Corrina"*

So now that you know the basics and have a couple of popular songs under your belt, it's time to check out these bonus videos on the DVD to learn some more chords, fun chord progressions, and a cool guitar riff – take your playing to the next level!

VIDEO: *watch Video 26 "C Major Chord"*
watch Video 27 "A Minor Chord"
watch Video 28 "E Minor Chord"
watch Video 29 "Making Music (half speed)"
watch Video 30 "Making Music"
watch Video 31 "Riff 1"
watch Video 32 "GCD Jam"

iPlayMusic®

Beginner Guitar Lessons
STYLES
Rock, Blues, Country, Metal and Punk

Barre Chords

VIDEO: *watch Video 33 "Warm Up"*

Barre (pronounced "bar") chords open up a whole new world of possibilities. Once you learn the basic barre chord shapes, you will know how to play many chords in many different positions on the neck, because barre chords sound great no matter where you play them.

Barre chord 1

Barre chord 1 uses the entire fretboard, all six strings. In constructing these types of chords, you will press down on multiple strings with just one finger. This technique of pressing down on multiple strings with one finger is called "barring."

To construct barre chord one, follow these **seven steps:**

1. Lay your **first finger**, your index finger, across all the strings (strings 6 through 1) on the 3rd fret and press down firmly across the entire fretboard.

2. **Play** the strings one at a time to make sure that the strings are not buzzing against the frets and that all the strings are ringing out.

3. Place your **second finger** on the third string, 4th fret.

4. Place your **third finger** on the fifth string, 5th fret.

5. Place your **fourth finger** on the fourth string, 5th fret.

6. **Play** each individual string again and make sure that each string rings out and you don't hear any fret buzz.

7. **Practice** playing this chord with strumming pattern 1 (from the Basics lessons).

If at any time you are getting frustrated, don't get discouraged. Take each of these steps, **one at a time**, have patience, **practice** slowly, and gradually build up strength in your hand to play this chord. Remember to practice the finger strength exercise from Basics. This will help you to build strength and coordination in both your right and left hands.

In **figure 1**, you see the shape of the barre chord. Notice that the first finger is pressing firmly across all the strings.

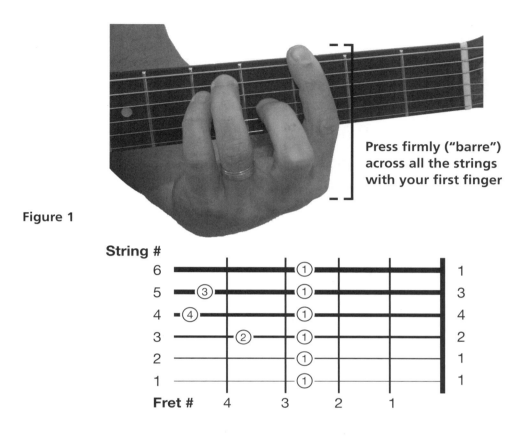

Figure 1

Press firmly ("barre") across all the strings with your first finger

One of the most challenging aspects of this chord for most beginners is barring across all six strings and pressing down firmly enough, so that all the strings ring out, and you don't hear any fret buzz. The key to getting a **nice full sound** is to use your **thumb** to press firmly into the back of the neck against your first finger, so that all the strings ring out and sound good. As you are building this chord, your hand may get tired from the constant pressure that you must apply with your first finger in order to get a nice full sound.

Press firmly with your thumb into the back of the neck

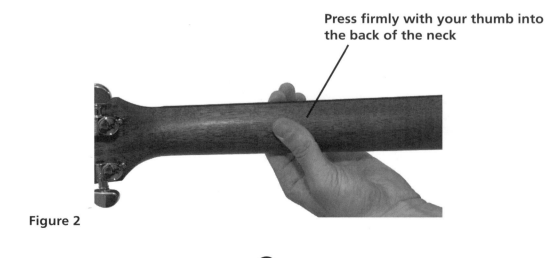

Figure 2

Barre Chords

Remember to take breaks and build up slowly. This chord requires **hand strength**, which you are gradually building.

VIDEO: *watch Video 34 "Barre Chord 1"*
  watch Video 35 "Practicing Barre Chord 1"

Barre chord 2

Barre chord 2 is a different shape than barre chord 1. With this chord you will barre with your first finger and your third finger.

To construct barre chord 2, follow these **six steps:**

1. Lay your **first finger**, your index finger, across strings 5 through 1 on the third fret and press down firmly across the fretboard.

2. **Play** the strings one at a time to make sure that the frets are not buzzing and that all the strings are ringing out.

3. Lay your **third finger** across strings 4, 3, and 2 on the fifth fret.

4. **Play** each individual string again and make sure that each string rings out and you don't hear any fret buzz.

5. **Practice** playing this chord with strumming pattern 1 (from the Basics lessons).

6. Make sure you do not play the sixth string.

In **figure 3**, you see the shape of the barre chord. Notice how you barre with both the first and the third fingers.

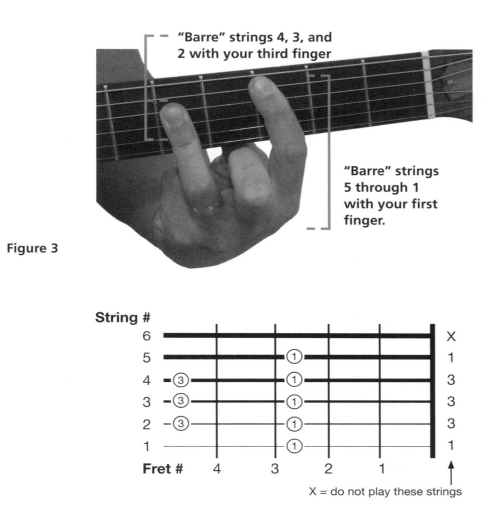

"Barre" strings 4, 3, and 2 with your third finger

"Barre" strings 5 through 1 with your first finger.

Figure 3

X = do not play these strings

VIDEO: *watch Video 36 "Barre Chord 2"*
watch Video 37 "Practicing Barre Chord 2"

Moving Barre Chords Around

The beauty of barre chords is that once you have learned the basic shape, you can move this same shape **up and down the neck**, and it sounds great no matter where you play it.

Try moving both **Barre Chord 1** and **Barre Chord 2** up and down the neck, and notice that they both sound good no matter where you play them.

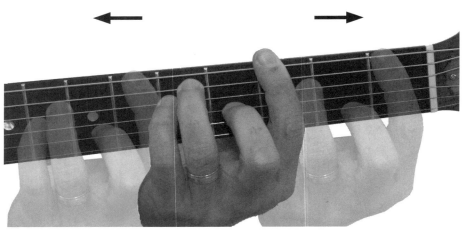

Figure 4

VIDEO: *watch Video 38 "Moving Barre Chords Around"*

Special note: The two barre chords we have just learned are major barre chords. As you move them up and down the neck, what you are doing is playing a different major chord each time. Here are some examples of the names of the chords you are playing as you move your hand up and down the neck:

Barre Chord 1

First finger is on the...	Name of the chord is...
First fret	F Major
Third fret	G Major
Fifth fret	A Major

Barre Chord 2

First finger is on the...	Name of the chord is...
Second fret	B Major
Third fret	C Major
Fifth fret	D Major

The rest of this book is dedicated to teaching you different styles of playing guitar. We chose **rock, blues, country, metal and punk,** because these apply well to the guitar, and you often hear elements of these different styles mixed together, even within the same song. Rock is based on blues, metal and punk are based on rock, and country and folk elements are at the heart of a **countless number of popular songs** that incorporate blues, rock, and even metal and punk styles. So, even if you only love one of these four genres, it is well worth it to learn something about each of them, because music and songs are **melting pots** of ideas, often crossing over genres and boundaries.

In the following sections, the **videos will become much more important** for your learning, because for each style, we have created a step-by-step sequence of videos that, in combination with this book, are designed to get you playing the "jams" and songs as quickly as possible.

You should approach each of these sections as follows:

1. **Scan once** quickly through the section and pick up what you can.

2. Make sure to **watch** any new chord **videos** for that section that you will need to learn before the first strumming video.

3. **Watch** the first **strumming video** and play along.

4. **Return** to the book and read through the explanation of the strumming pattern once more.

5. **Watch** the strumming video again.

6. **Watch** the transition video.

7. **Practice** transitioning between chords with the new strumming pattern.

8. When you have practiced and you feel comfortable, watch the "jam" video and **jam along** with the instructor.

Rhythm and "Feel"

Rhythm and "feel" is something that you really need to see and hear. For that reason, we strongly recommend that you **watch the videos** to learn how we suggest each strumming pattern within each style should be played. If you find you're having trouble understanding this material, the videos will allow you to **see and hear** the rhythm while playing along with the instructor, which is extremely useful in developing your own sense of rhythm and feel.

Styles

Our approach to teaching rhythm and feel in the book is to use **numbers and your own voice**. Broadly speaking, each style has a signature rhythm or "feel" that makes it recognizable. In describing this typical feel for each style, we've listed the numbers "1-2-3-4" under the title of each section. This indicates which beats are emphasized in a four-beat pattern.

Count out loud "one, two, three, four" at a steady tempo over and over, and then say a number louder or softer depending on whether or not it is underlined. When a number is underlined, that means it should be emphasized (say it louder).

This 1-2-3-4 rhythm and feel guideline is listed below each style title as well as under the arrows that describe each strumming pattern. **As you are strumming these patterns on your guitar,** try to emphasize or de-emphasize the up- and downstrokes for each strumming pattern (strum the strings harder or softer) depending on what the recommended feel is.

Special Note: In Basics you were first introduced to the concept of strumming patterns. Following is a refresher on some of the terminology and symbols used in this book to describe strumming patterns:

A **strumming pattern** consists of downstrokes and upstrokes.

A **downstroke** is played by strumming the guitar strings from the top of the guitar to the bottom – or from the 6th (low E) string to the 1st (high E) string. We will represent a downstroke with a down arrow.

An **upstroke** is played by strumming the guitar strings from the bottom of the guitar to the top – or from the 1st (high E) string to the 6th (low E) string. We will represent an upstroke with an up arrow:

Remember to think of your strumming hand as a windshield wiper, or a pendulum. A **dashed arrow** will represent the direction your arm should be moving as you swing your arm up and down without hitting the strings.

If arrows are spaced equally apart from each other, then you will keep your strumming hand moving up and down in a steady, even motion.

If arrows are spaced closer together and further apart, such as with a pattern that has a **swing** feel, try adjusting your arm swing to give the pattern a swing feel (if you have difficulty swinging the pattern just by reading the book, make sure to **watch the videos first**).

1 <u>2</u> 3 <u>4</u>

New Chords

F Major

VIDEO: *watch Video 39 "F Major Chord"*

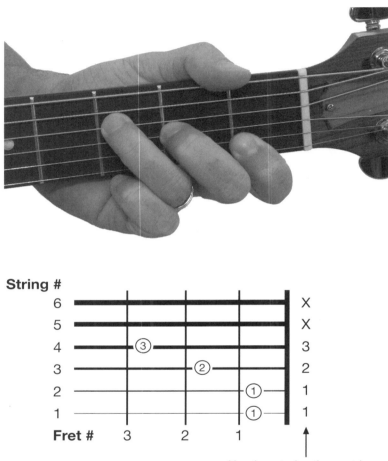

Figure 5

Rock lesson one

CHORDS USED IN THIS LESSON:

- C Major (taught in Basics)
- F Major

Rock rhythms typically emphasize the second and fourth beats. This is often referred to as "backbeat." **Practice** saying out loud "one, two, three, four," saying "two" and "four" louder and putting an equal **emphasis** on the "two" and the "four."

Strumming pattern: Down, down, up, down, down, up, up, down, up, down.

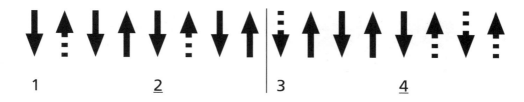

Once you've mastered rock strumming pattern 1, it's time to move on to the transition. Make sure to nail the F Major chord, the strumming pattern, and the transition, before playing along with the jam video.

VIDEO: *watch Video 40 "Rock Strumming 1"*
          watch Video 41 "Rock Transition 1"
          watch Video 42 "Rock Jam 1"

Blues

1 <u>2</u> 3 <u>4</u>

New Chords

A7

VIDEO: *watch Video 43 "A7 Chord"*

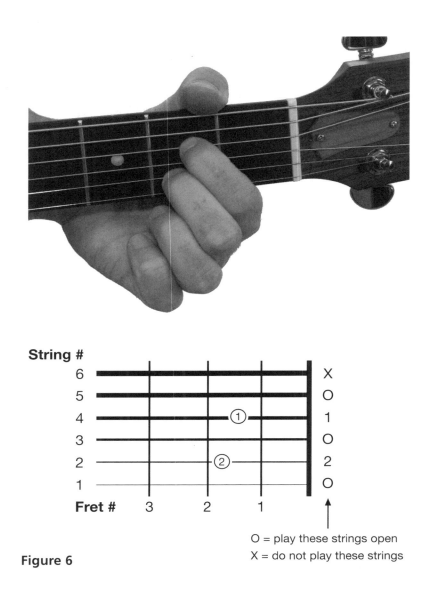

Figure 6

O = play these strings open
X = do not play these strings

D7

VIDEO: *watch Video 44 "D7 Chord"*

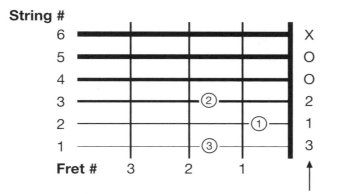

O = play these strings open
X = do not play these strings

Figure 7

E Major

VIDEO: *watch Video 45 "E Major Chord"*

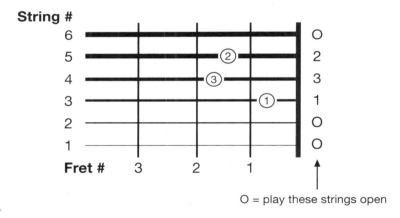

O = play these strings open

Figure 8

E7

VIDEO: *watch Video 46 "E7 Chord"*

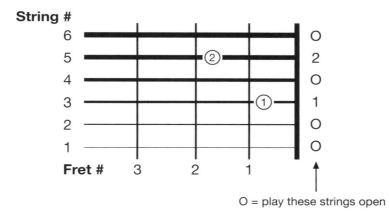

O = play these strings open

Figure 9

Blues

Blues lesson one

CHORDS USED IN THIS LESSON:

- A7
- D7
- E7

Like rock rhythms, blues rhythms typically also emphasize beats 2 and 4. Blues is often played at a slower tempo than rock, and may also have more of a "swing" feel.

Swing

Blues strumming pattern 1 has a nice swing feel. What do we mean by "swing" feel? Imagine yourself swinging back and forth on a real swing. The feeling of swinging forward and backward, hanging suspended in the air, accelerating down as you head towards earth and then being suspended in air again is similar to the **lagging and pushing** sensation from a musical swing feel. Now try swinging your strumming arm up and down, rather than moving your arm at the exact same steady pace like a windshield wiper. Incorporating this muscle control into your strumming is how to achieve the swing feel.

Figure 10

VIDEO: *watch video 47 "Swing Feel"*

Strumming pattern: Down, down, down, up, up, down, down.

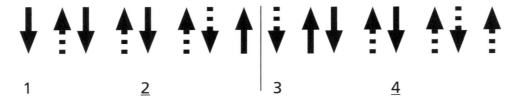

1   2   3   4

Special note: Often to keep strumming patterns interesting, artists will use a **"call and response"** technique, where the first half of a pattern is fairly straightforward, and the second half is a "response" or variation on the first half. Even though the second half of the pattern may be different than the first half to add variation, the overall feel of the pattern is still the same. In this case, the bluesy swing **feel** pervades, and there is a variation in the second half of the pattern.

VIDEO: *watch Video 48 "Blues Strumming 1"*
watch Video 49 "Blues Transition 1"
watch Video 50 "Blues Jam 1"

<u>1</u> 2 <u>3</u> 4

Country lesson one

CHORDS USED IN THIS LESSON:

- A Minor (taught in Basics)
- C Major (taught in Basics)
- F Major
- G Major (taught in Basics)

Country rhythms will often emphasize beats 1 and 3 which makes the music feel "upbeat." Rhythm guitar strumming patterns in country music often emphasize the lower bass notes on the 1 and 3 and the high notes on the 2 and 4 (which fills in the rhythm nicely and gives the music a nice upbeat feeling).

Special note: Country strumming pattern 1 also has a swing feel. For a refresher on swing, re-read the Blues section, which describes how to incorporate swing into your strumming.

Strumming pattern: Down, down, up, down, down, up

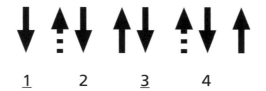

<u>1</u>   2   <u>3</u>   4

Make sure to nail all the chords, the strumming pattern, and the transition, before playing along with the jam video.

VIDEO: *Watch Video 51 "Country Strumming 1"*
Watch Video 52 "Country Transition 1"
Watch Video 53 "Country Jam 1"

<u>1</u> <u>2</u> <u>3</u> <u>4</u>

Power Chords

Power chords are the standard weapons of choice among metal and punk guitarists. Just like barre chords, power chords have the characteristic of sounding good no matter where you position them on the guitar neck. Once you learn the basic power chord shape, you can move it up and down the neck, and it sounds good no matter where you play it.

In figures 11 and 12, you see the shape and construction of power chords 1 and 2 using three fingers. Just like barre chords, power chord shapes can be moved up and down the neck, and they sound great. You can think of these as "stripped down" versions of barre chords. The 3-finger versions are just the first three notes (the top section) of a barre chord shape. NOTE: This chord can also be played with just fingers 1 and 3. There are a few reasons why these chords are used a lot in metal and punk:

- You can play them fast
- You can play them hard
- You can play them with lots of distortion and they sound great (on electric guitar)

Power Chord 1 (3 fingers)

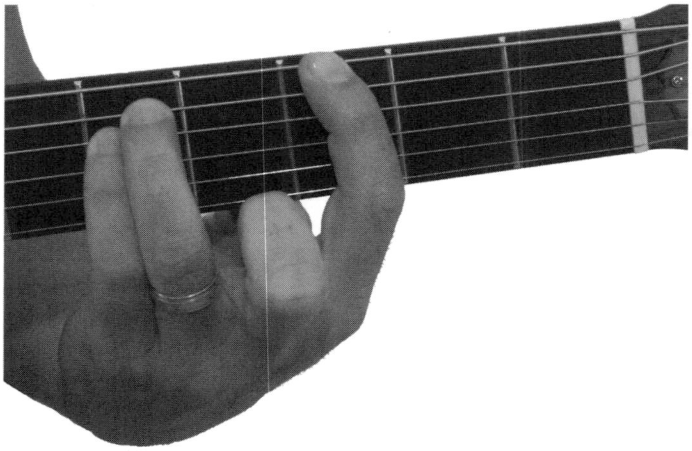

Figure 11

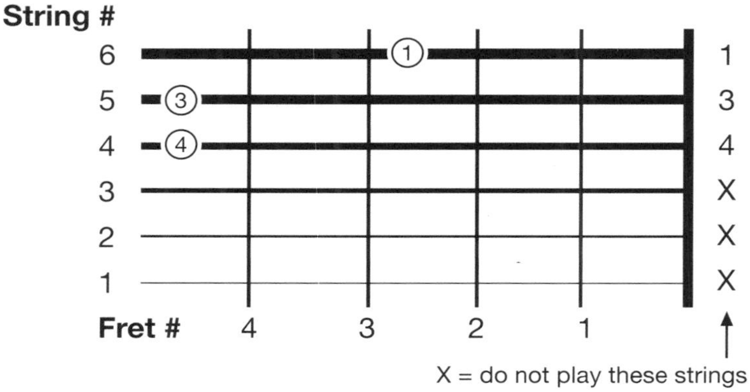

X = do not play these strings

Power Chord 2 (3 fingers)

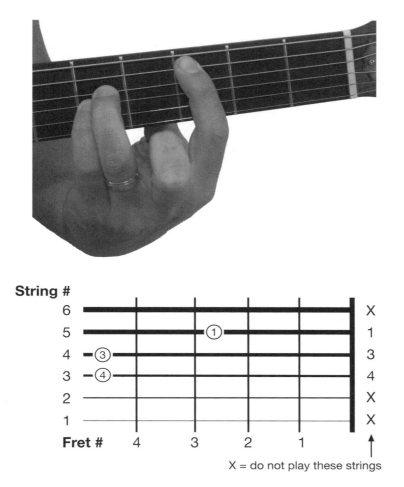

Figure 12

String #

6					X
5			①		1
4	③				3
3	④				4
2					X
1					X

Fret #   4   3   2   1   ↑

X = do not play these strings

Muting

In strumming a power chord, you have two basic options: play it muted, or play it open.

Muting is a technique in which you lay the side of your strumming hand across the strings near the bridge of the guitar, and then strum the guitar while maintaining your hand position.

Metal & Punk

Figures 13 and 14 illustrate how you mute the strings while strumming with the same hand. Playing muted power chords is common in many genres of music, and it is perhaps most predominant in metal, although it is used quite a bit in punk as well. If you are looking for a "chunky" sound that is extremely **rhythmic and precise**, then muting is a great way to do that.

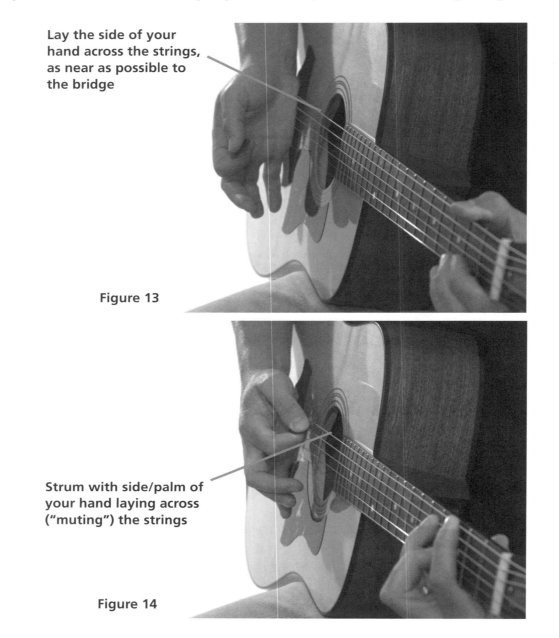

Lay the side of your hand across the strings, as near as possible to the bridge

Figure 13

Strum with side/palm of your hand laying across ("muting") the strings

Figure 14

The other option in playing power chords is to play them open rather than muting them. This sound is more common in punk, where the precision that you can achieve with muting is not as important. If you are looking for a hard, thrashy, slightly disorganized sound, then open power chords might be the right choice.

VIDEO: *watch Video 54 "Power Chord 1"*
watch Video 55 "Muting Power Chord 1"
watch Video 56 "Power Chord 2"

Metal & Punk lesson one

CHORDS USED IN THIS LESSON:

- Power Chord 1
- Power Chord 2

Although metal and punk is probably more accurately considered an extension of rock, where the emphasis is on beats 2 and 4, the music is often played so hard that it seems like every beat is emphasized.

Strumming pattern: Down, down, down, down

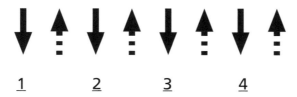

Once you've mastered metal strumming pattern 1, it's time to move on to the transitions. Make sure to nail the muting technique, all the chords, the strumming pattern, and the transitions, before playing along with the jam video.

VIDEO: *watch Video 57 "Metal Strumming 1"*
watch Video 58 "Metal Transition 1"
watch Video 59 "Metal Transition 2"
watch Video 60 "Metal Jam 1"

Songs

FIRST SONG

Midnight Special
Made popular by Creedence Clearwater Revival,
Leadbelly, and Hoyt Axton

This song is based on a real 1920's train, the "Midnight Special," which used to pass a Texas prison. The train was a symbol of hope for inmates, as it was the means by which relatives were brought to the prison for visits. A true American classic, "Midnight Special" has been adapted and recorded successfully as a blues, country, folk, and rock & roll song.

VIDEO: *watch videos 61-64 "Midnight Special"*

SECOND SONG

Salty Dog
Made popular by Johnny Cash
and Mississippi John Hurt

Although its origins are unknown, "Salty Dog" has been a standard for blues, folk and bluegrass performers for decades. A humorous song, the "Salty Dog" references "low-life" characters and their sometimes less-than-noble behavior.

VIDEO: *watch videos 65-68 "Salty Dog"*

THIRD SONG

Will the Circle Be Unbroken
Made popular by Willie Nelson,
The Carter Family, and Nitty Gritty Dirt Band

First published in 1907, "Will the Circle Be Unbroken" is one of America's most beloved (and recorded) songs. With its spiritual lyrics, "Will the Circle Be Unbroken" speaks to universal themes of loss, grief, salvation, and hope.

VIDEO: *watch videos 69-72 "Will the Circle Be Unbroken"*

A Major

VIDEO: *watch Video 8 "A Major Chord"*

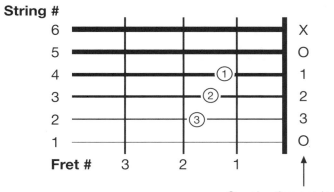

O = play these strings open
X = do not play these strings

Chords

C Major

VIDEO: *watch Video 26 "C Major Chord"*

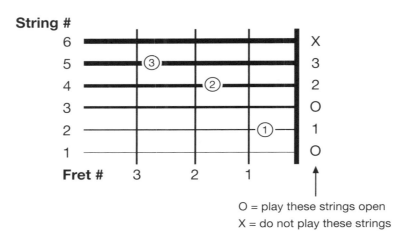

O = play these strings open
X = do not play these strings

D Major

VIDEO: *watch Video 10 "D Major Chord"*

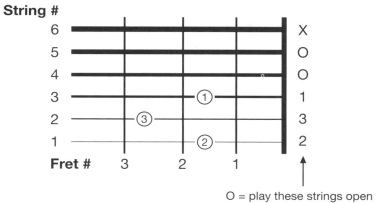

O = play these strings open
X = do not play these strings

E Major

VIDEO: *watch Video 45 "E Major Chord"*

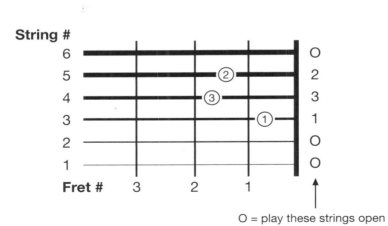

O = play these strings open

F Major

VIDEO: *watch Video 39 "F Major Chord"*

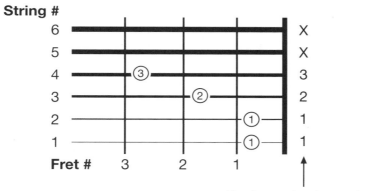

X = do not play these strings

G Major

VIDEO: *watch Video 9 "G Major Chord"*

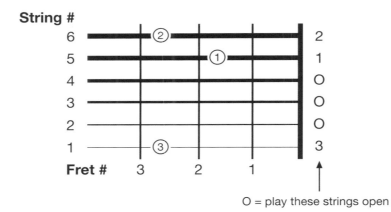

O = play these strings open

A7

VIDEO: *watch Video 43 "A7 Chord"*

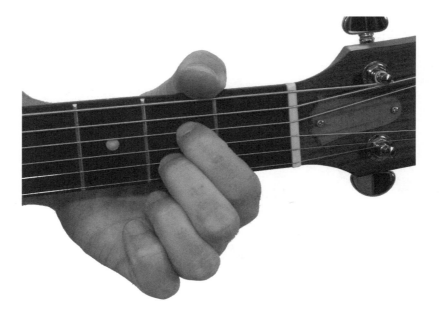

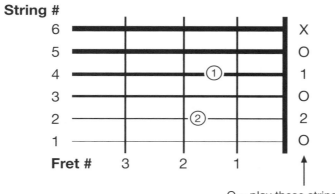

O = play these strings open
X = do not play these strings

D7

VIDEO: *watch Video 44 "D7 Chord"*

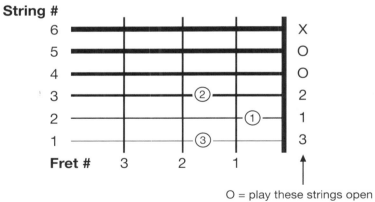

String #

		Fret #		
6				X
5				O
4				O
3		②		2
2			①	1
1			③	3

Fret #   3   2   1

O = play these strings open
X = do not play these strings

E7

VIDEO: *watch Video 46 "E7 Chord"*

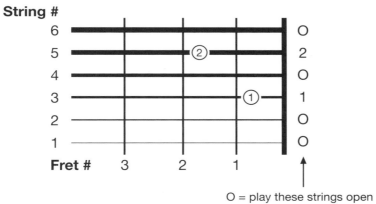

O = play these strings open

G7

VIDEO: *watch Video 78 "G7 Chord"*

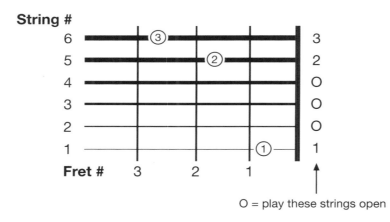

O = play these strings open

A Minor

VIDEO: *watch Video 27 "A Minor Chord"*

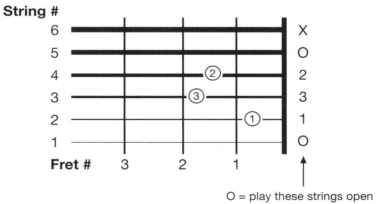

O = play these strings open
X = do not play these strings

D Minor

VIDEO: *watch Video 77 "D Minor Chord"*

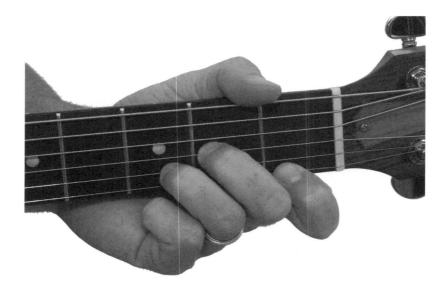

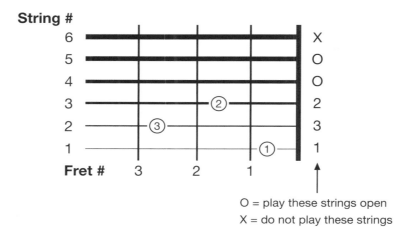

O = play these strings open
X = do not play these strings

E Minor

VIDEO: *watch Video 28 "E Minor Chord"*

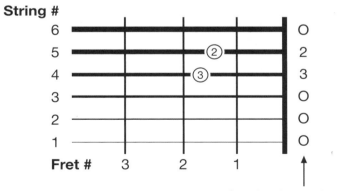

O = play these strings open

Chords

Barre Chord 1

VIDEO: *watch Video 34 "Barre Chord 1"*

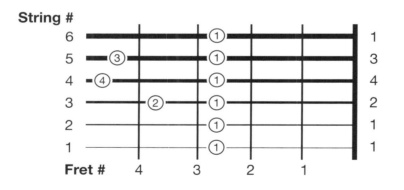

Barre Chord 2

VIDEO: *watch Video 36 "Barre Chord 2"*

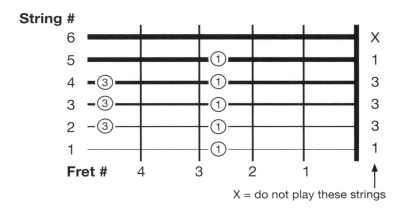

X = do not play these strings

Chords

Power Chord 1

VIDEO: *watch Video 54 "Power Chord 1"*

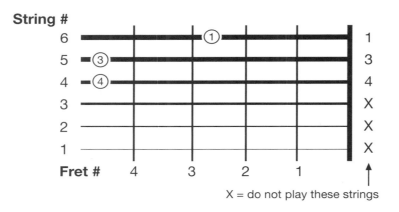

String #

6			①			1
5	③					3
4	④					4
3						X
2						X
1						X

Fret #   4   3   2   1

X = do not play these strings

Power Chord 2

VIDEO: *watch Video 56 "Power Chord 2"*

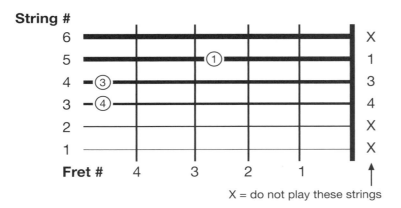

X = do not play these strings

Next Steps

So now that you know how to play some songs, and you've developed your rock, blues, country, metal and punk guitar skills, it's time to check out the bonus videos, which will give you even more chords, cool guitar riffs, and fun progressions to play around with.

VIDEO: *watch Video 73 "Riff 1 Expanded"*
watch Video 74 "A Major Alternate Fingering"
watch Video 75 "Riff 2 – Rock"
watch Video 76 "Riff 3 – Mellow"
watch Video 77 "D Minor Chord"
watch Video 78 "G7 Chord"
watch Video 79 "Stringing the Guitar"

Remember to check back at our website often: **http://www.iPlayMusic.com**

We are working hard right now to develop more song-based videos and learning materials to help you learn more popular songs and develop more advanced techniques. Stay tuned for many more exciting products to come!

Thank you for purchasing Beginner Guitar Lessons from iPlayMusic. On behalf of the entire iPlayMusic team, we wish you success in your newfound passion! We would love to hear from you and value **your feedback**. Please send us your comments and any ideas you might have for additional instructional tools and videos: **feedback@iplaymusic.com**